THE COOLEST CHINESE

Natural Wonders

Jill Keppeler

CRAZY COOL CHINA

ROSEN PUBLISHING
NEW YORK

SinolinguA
华语教学出版社
BEIJING

Published in 2023 by The Rosen Publishing Group, Inc.
2544 Clinton St, Buffalo, NY 14224

Jointly published in 2023 by Sinolingua Co.,Ltd., Beijing, China, and The Rosen Publishing Group, Inc., New York, New York, United States.

First Edition

Editor: Jill Keppeler
Designer: Rachel Rising

Photo credits: Cover, p. 5 aphotostory/Shutterstock.com; Cover, pp.1-48 Sylfida/Shuttterstock.com; pp. 4, 6, 10, 14, 18, 22, 26, 30, 34, 38, 42 Elina Li/Shutterstock.com; p. 7 TonyV3112/Shutterstock.com; p. 8 Efired/Shutterstock.com; p. 11 Rigamondis/Shuttterstock.com; p. 12 Ana Flasker/Shutterstock.com; pp. 15, 35 martinho Smart/Shutterstock.com; p. 16 Guosheng Wu/Shutterstock.com; p. 19 Sean Pavone/Shutterstock.com; p. 20 JingAiping/Shuttterstock.com; p. 23 SJ Travel Photo and Video/Shutterstock.com; p. 24 naturesharing/Shutterstock.com; p. 27 aaron choi/Shutterstock.com; p. 28 Moolkum/Shutterstock.com; p. 31 Wirestock Creators/Shutterstock.com; p. 32 https://en.wikipedia.org/wiki/File:View_1_in_Snowy_Jade_Cave,_Fengdu_County.JPG; p. 36 chinahbzyg/Shutterstock.com; p. 39 54613/Shutterstock.com; p. 40 Dimdok/Shutterstock.com; p. 43 James Jiao/Shutterstock.com.

Names: Keppeler, Jill
Title: The coolest chinese natural wonders / Jill Keppeler.
Description: New York : Rosen Publishing, 2023. | Series: Crazy Cool China | Includes bibliographic information, glossary and index.
Identifiers: ISBN 9781499474664 (pbk) | ISBN 9781499474671 (library bound) | ISBN 9781499474688 (ebook)
Subjects: LCSH: China- Juvenile literature | Geography- Juvenile literature | World Heritage sites- Juvenile literature
Classification: LCC DS706.7 K47 2023 | DDC 951 -dc23

Manufactured in the United States of America

CPSIA Compliance Information: Batch #CWRYA24. For further information, contact Rosen Publishing, New York, New York, at 1-800-237-9932.

Contents

A Land of Great Contrasts

China is one of the largest countries in the world—covering a land area of about 3.7 million square miles (9.6 million sq km)—so it's not so surprising that it contains a huge variety of natural wonders. Those millions of miles contain a **diverse** range of natural relief and climates, with many **ecological** niches, varied landforms, and geological extremes. It's a land of enormous contrasts, too, with some of the highest and lowest points on Earth as well as immense differences in temperature.

China has many man-made wonders as well. The Great Wall is perhaps the most well-known (and largest), sprawling thousands of miles across the country. However, the terracotta army of Shaanxi Province, the Leshan Buddha of Leshan City, and more modern wonders such as the Three Gorges Dam are also worth a look.

Accordingly, the country's natural wonders include mountains and canyons, forests and deserts. Some wonders have to do with waterways and bodies of water, including the ocean—China has about 11,120 miles (18,000 km) of coastline along the Pacific Ocean. Some (such as the Shilin, or stone forest) defy description. But they all have one thing in common: they're all incredible examples of the diversity and beauty of our planet Earth.

China is the third-largest country in the world by area. Only Russia and Canada are bigger.

Lakes of Many Colors

The largest saltwater lake in China lies more than 10,000 feet (3,048 m) over sea level, nestled in the Qilian Mountains in west-central China. Qinghai Lake (also called Blue Lake or Koko Nor) has, unsurprisingly, deep blue waters that can reach nearly 100 feet (30.5 m) deep. It's right in the middle of many of the region's bird **migration** paths, and Bird Island, located in its northwest corner, is a breeding ground for thousands of species of birds.

People have harvested salt from Yuncheng Lake (called "China's Dead Sea" for how salty it is) for at least 6,000 years. At one point, it was responsible for about a quarter of China's salt production.

Yuncheng Lake (also called Xiechi Lake) in Shanxi Province isn't as large as Qinghai Lake, but it makes up for that in variety. In summer, blooms of a certain type of algae produce different **pigments**, turning the lake many different colors including green, magenta, red, and purple. And in the winter, the salt in the lake forms crystals that make the scene sparkle.

Buddhist travelers sometimes circle the entire Qinghai Lake as a form of **pilgrimage**.

Jiuzhaigou National Park is notable for many reasons. A number of rare animals and plants live in the region, and it's a **UNESCO** World **Heritage** site (one of China's dozens) and a World Biosphere Reserve.

In Sichuan Province, Jiuzhaigou National Park is also known for its colorful nature. The park was one of the first in the country, and it has more than 100 lakes, as well as many waterfalls, forests, and other features. There are nine Tibetan villages within the park, which is a valley in the Min Mountains.

Long Lake is the deepest of the park's lakes and the one at the highest elevation. It's known for its blue and green shades. Five Colors Pond nearby is one of the smallest of the park's bodies of water but has some of the richest colors. Other notable lakes in Jiuzhaigou include Panda Lake, Five Flower Lake, Mirror Lake, and Sleeping Dragon Lake.

Autumn colors contrast with the blue-green colors of Jiuzhaigou National Park's Five Flower Lake.

Above the Clouds

Perhaps one of the most famous natural sites (and sights) in eastern China is Huangshan, Yellow Mountain. This range has inspired poets and artists for thousands of years. The steep mountain peaks loom over the **atmospheric** fog, creating the **illusion** that they're rising above a sea of clouds.

Huangshan, another UNESCO World Heritage site, inspired an entire school of landscape painting called *shanshui*, or "mountain and water," starting in the 16th century. It's been called "the loveliest mountain of China."

Huangshan is partly known for its "four wonders," which include its uniquely shaped rocks, its cloud sea, its hot springs, and the ancient, twisted, tough pine trees that grow while clinging to the peaks. Today, visitors can take a cable car from the base of the mountain to its summit. It's also a popular hiking spot.

While the famous pine trees are perhaps Huangshan's most well-known plants, the mountain has a huge diversity of plant life, including many ferns.

The mountains of Zhangye Danxia have many colors, and sometimes the light on the rocks adds even more.

It's said that there are five great mountains of China: Mount Heng in Hunan Province, Mount Heng in Shanxi Province, Mount Song in Henan Province, Mount Tai in Shandong Province, and Mount Hua in Shaanxi Province.

Zhangye Danxia National Geological Park in Gansu Province is home to China's "Rainbow Mountain." Mineral deposits have piled up over millions of years to create colorful layers in the rock formations. Weathering and erosion have further worn the formations into strange and oddly beautiful shapes such as pillars and ravines.

About one-third of the land in China is mountainous. The country claims the tallest mountain in the world: Mount Qomolangma (known as Mount Everest in the West), which lies on the border between China and Nepal. It reaches a height of more than 29,000 feet (8,839 m) and is part of the great Himalayas of southern Asia. Hundreds of people attempt to climb Qomolangma every year—and several die each year in the attempt. Glaciers cover the mountain's slopes, and temperatures even during the warmest time of year in the region only average about -2 degrees Fahrenheit (-19 degrees Celsius).

Lowest of the Low

The high-altitude points of China are matched by its lows. The country has one of the lowest points in the world—the dried-up Lake Ayding in the Turpan depression in Xinjiang. It's 505 feet (153.9 m) below sea level. Only the Dead Sea and the Sea of Galilee and Lac Assal are lower.

Tiger Leaping Gorge is known for its popular and famous hiking trail. The gorge has three parts—upper, middle, and lower—but the high gorge tends to be the most popular with hikers and tourists.

That's extreme, but China also has many gorges and ravines to match its high peaks. Tiger Leaping Gorge in southwest China is the deepest of its kind in the world, with an altitude difference of more than 12,000 feet (3,657.8 m) between the bottom and the peaks around it. The Jinsha River makes its way through the bottom of the gorge. The gorge has a connected legend of how it got its name. This story says a tiger escaped from a hunter by leaping to safety from one side of the gorge to the other.

The Jinsha River at the bottom of Tiger Leaping Gorge is a **tributary** of the Yangtze River.

People have lived on the Loess Plateau for a very long time. Loess can become very fertile soil, and the region once fed many people in the country. However, over time, erosion and overfarming have degraded the soil. Today, many people are working to reverse the trend.

The Loess Plateau takes up about 154,000 square miles (398,858 sq km) in north-central China. While the plateau averages about 4,000 feet (1,219 m) in elevation, it's covered with deep ravines and gorges that cut into the earth. In fact, these gashes may take up half of the entire region.

This phenomenon results from the plateau's namesake—loess, a yellow-brown, mineral-rich material often carried by wind or glaciers. It can lie more than 250 feet (76.2 m) deep on the plateau. This loess is very susceptible to erosion by water today, leading to its many ravines.

Erosion has cut gashes that are hundreds of feet deep into the Loess Plateau.

Karst Landscapes

Karst is a type of region that's made up of limestone. Because limestone is a relatively soft rock that can be easily worn away by water, karst landscapes can be many interesting shapes. Water can wear the stone away from the top down or from the inside out. There may be cliffs, caves, or underground streams. There may also be sinkholes, holes in the ground worn away from the surface rock.

The Yangshuo region draws many tourists who enjoy bicycling through the area. The trip from Yangshuo village to Moon Hill takes about 40 minutes. Another popular peak in the region is Green Lotus Peak.

The village of Yangshuo is, of course, man-made, and it's very popular with tourists (particularly backpackers) for its history and hiking trails. But a big part of this allure is because of the natural karst landscape around it. The limestone peaks are covered in lush greenery, and the Li River curls nearby. Moon Hill may be the area's most familiar and popular karst formation; this natural arch was once a limestone cave.

Moon Hill rises over the greenery in the Yangshuo region. Visitors can climb to the arch or the summit.

Lights turn the interior of Furong cave many colors.

There are three main karst landform styles, including *fenglin*, which are tower formations; *fengcong*, which are cone formations; and *shilin*, which are stone forest formations.

The South China Karst is a UNESCO World Heritage site that spans four provinces of China, including the region in which Yangshuo and Moon Hill are located. It includes many parks with karst formations. Another of this site's notable features is the Ten Thousand Peaks Forest in Guizhou Province, which features many karst peaks, waterfalls, and cave networks. It's also called Wanfenglin. The "forest" of peaks is near Xingyi and takes up about 772 square miles (1,999.5 sq km)—nearly twice as big as New York City.

Wulong in Chongqing is also part of the heritage site. This location is known in part for its dolines, or sinkholes. One notable site is Furong Cave, which is more than 9,000 feet (2,743.2 m) long and has many waterfalls and other features.

The Stone Forest

Perhaps the most unique and well-known karst formation in China (and the world) is the Stone Forest, or Shilin, near Kunming in Yunnan Province. Parts of this site are also part of the South China Karst. Over a span of about 186 square miles (481.7 sq km), hundreds of limestone pillars shaped by wind and water rise over **terrain** that includes caves, ponds, and lakes. Some look like cones or columns; others resemble animals or plants.

Every year, many tourists visit the Stone Forest. Busloads visit from nearby Kunming, including both tour groups and more solitary travelers. It can get crowded! Visitors should plan on spending at least three to four hours at the site.

The formations of the Stone Forest are more than 200 million years old. The region was once a huge, shallow ocean, but as Earth changed over the centuries, the seabed rose to many feet over sea level.

The stone, thick with fossil material, was then shaped by weather into the unique shapes it has today. Some pillars in the "forest" are sharp and pointed, while others are rounded into mushroom-like shapes.

Shilin includes both the Greater and Lesser Stone Forests and other areas.

Other features of the Stone Forest include an underground river and many waterfalls. People have given many of the rocks and other features their own names, such as Lotus Peak, Sword Peak Pond, Hanging Rock, and Strange Wind Cave.

One legend about the Stone Forest holds that, many years ago, Ashima, a woman of the **indigenous** Sani people who live near the site, was forbidden to marry the man she loved. She ran into the forest, where she was turned into a stone pillar rather than be forced to marry someone else. This stone still bears her name. Some versions of the legend say that Ashima was kidnapped by another man who wanted to marry her. She escaped but drowned in a flood and was turned into a stone pillar.

The Sani people celebrate a Torch Festival every year in June at the Stone Forest. This festival features many dances and competitions.

Ashima Rock in the Stone Forest is said to look like a woman with a **kerchief** on her head.

Otherworldly Beauty

Even if you've never visited China, you may think you've seen parts of Zhangjiajie National Park somewhere. That's because the 2009 movie *Avatar* was partly inspired by this beautiful, unique region. The mountains of the planet Pandora, on which the movie was set, were created on film by designers who studied the rock pillars of the park. Footage of the Southern Sky Column in particular was edited into the movie as the Hallelujah Mountains.

Of course, the park's 3,000 or so pillars are firmly rooted to the ground, unlike Pandora's mountains. However, fog often rises around the formations, creating an illusion of floating. Unlike those in karst landscapes, they're not limestone. Rather, they're quartz sandstone eroded by rain. The region is also full of ravines, canyons, and caves.

The Southern Sky Column (or rather, Avatar Hallelujah Mountain) stretches more than 3,500 feet (1,067 m) into the air.

The Zhangjiajie glass bridge was once the longest and highest in the world.

Some people are concerned that the sheer number of people visiting Zhangjiajie National Park will damage the site's beautiful scenery. The area has become more developed and **commercialized** over the years.

The national park consists of about 18.6 square miles (48 sq km), part of the greater Wulingyuan area, which is a UNESCO World Heritage site of about 153.5 square miles (398 sq km). Dense greenery lies over the terrain, including thousands of plant species, thanks to the wet climate. Many rare animals also live there.

More than 30 million tourists visit the Zhangjiajie park each year. Several man-made structures have been created to better entertain them as well. In 2016, the Zhangjiajie glass bridge opened, allowing visitors to walk out over the park. The huge Bailong

Subterranean

Many of China's more towering, majestic landforms are matched (often at the same site) by subterranean, or underground, wonders. Karst landscapes often have caves and sinkholes, such as Furong Cave, mentioned earlier. These can contain further wonders in their plants and wildlife, and many people are beginning to realize their potential for tourism (though that comes with problems of its own).

Researchers measure the length of a cave by all its main caves, branches, and rivers. The longest cave system known is Mammoth Cave in Kentucky in the United States. This cave system is more than 425 miles (684 km) long.

One of the most notable caves of China is Shuanghe Cave, located in Guizhou Province. It's sometimes considered the longest cave in Asia. The cave is home to some endangered species, including cave shrimp and salamanders, and a number of unique fossils. It's nearly 150 miles (241.4 km) long (about as long as the U.S. state of New Jersey) and includes underground rivers, waterfalls, and many chambers.

The Shuanghe Cave is one of the longest in the world. There are more than 200 entrances.

Snow Jade Cave is on the north bank of the Yangtze River. It has three levels. Many of the cave's **stalactites** are pure white. There are many named, unique stone formations there, including the King Stone Flag and the Snow Jade Penguin.

The Miao Room, located in the Gebihe Cave system in the Guizhou province, is one of the world's largest underground chambers. It's about 1.3 million square feet (120,774 sq m), which is the size of about 22 football fields, and full of enormous **stalagmites**. It's about 325 feet (99 m) underground. In 2013, a team used lasers to map it and other cave systems. A jumbo jet would fit inside easily!

China's caves are beautiful on their own, but they've also provided a refuge of sorts for many plants that had become endangered as people deforested the surface of Earth. In the 2010s, researchers studied dozens of caves in China and discovered more than 400 plant species. Some of them are likely the only ones of their kind left thanks to their subterranean habitat.

Snow Jade Cave and its formations are young for a karst cave—only 55,000 to 80,000 years old.

Rushing Waters

China has many rivers flowing through it, but the greatest are the Yellow and Yangtze Rivers. The Yangtze (called Chang Jiang in China) is the longest river in China and Asia, as well as the third-longest river in the world. It stretches more than 3,900 miles (6,276 km) across the country, and more than a third of the population lives in its basin. It carries an enormous amount of water.

The Three Parallel Rivers region is very biologically diverse. It's home to more than 6,000 species of plants, more than 170 species of mammals, and more than 400 species of birds. Many of them are **endemic** and endangered.

In Yunnan Province, the river runs parallel with two other rivers, the Lancang River and the Nujiang River. They travel through gorges up to 9,842.5 feet (3,000 m) deep and among mountains up to 19,685 feet (6,000 m) high. (In fact, Tiger Leaping Gorge is in this area.) This Three Parallel Rivers region is a UNESCO World Heritage site.

The Yangtze River basin provides about half of all China's crops. These crops include rice, beans, wheat, and more.

It's common for rainbows to form over the Hukou Waterfall. Thousands of people visit it every year.

The largest waterfall in China is the Huangguoshu Waterfall on the Baishui River in Guizhou Province. It's more than 220 feet (67 m) tall and more than 270 feet (82.3 m) wide. There are also 17 smaller waterfalls in the national park around it.

The Yellow River, or Huang He, basin is considered China's cradle of civilization. It's important to Chinese folklore and written history, both for its major floods and its influence on the region's economy, culture, and agriculture. The river starts on the Qinghai-Tibet Plateau before it (and its tributaries) flows past some of the country's oldest cities. It ends at the Bohai Sea, part of the Yellow Sea.

One notable sight along the Yellow River is the Hukou Waterfall, located on the Loess Plateau, where the Shanxi and Shaanxi Provinces meet. It's one of the largest waterfalls in China and the world's largest yellow waterfall. Not long before the falls, the river suddenly decreases from about 440 yards (402.3 m) wide to about 55 yards (50.3 m) wide, the water turning into churning rapids before surging over the drop.

Living Wonders

Some of China's natural wonders are living and growing. The country has tens of thousands of plant species, including hundreds that are endemic. The wide variety of climates and terrain means there's also a wide variety of plant types, although there are two main areas: the wet, warm southeast and the drier northwest.

> Many animals also live at Red Beach, including hundreds of species of birds and mammals. One particular rare resident is the red-crowned crane. These birds get their name from a patch of red skin on their head.

While all this plant life is amazing in itself, the country also has a few plant-related sites that classify as wonders on their own. Red Beach in the Liaohe River delta, near Panjin, is part of one of the world's largest wetlands. It gets its name from the *Suaeda salsa* plants that flourish there in the **alkaline** soil. Every fall, they turn bright red, making it seem as though the area is some odd alien landscape.

Red Beach is in an environmentally protected area, but there are wooden walkways that extend out over the water so people can better see the view.

Mukeng Bamboo Forest includes three main scenic areas and a circular hiking trail. Xiu Nu Lake in the park often looks brilliant green with the bamboo reflected in its waters.

Parts of the 2000 movie *Crouching Tiger, Hidden Dragon* were filmed in the Shunan and Mukeng Bamboo Forests, as well as others. The movie was nominated for 10 Academy Awards in 2001.

The many plants collectively called bamboo have a large part in Chinese culture. Bamboo is a symbol of virtue and has played a role in artwork and poetry. The Chinese people have also used it for many things for more than 7,000 years—including food, housing, weapons, and even the first books. There are more than 16.3 million acres (6.6 million ha) of bamboo forests in China.

The largest and oldest bamboo forest in the country is Shunan Bamboo Forest, located in Sichuan Province. This forest covers about 46 square miles (119.1 sq km) and includes 27 mountains and more than 500 peaks. It also has more than 400 kinds of bamboo. Another is Mukeng Bamboo Forest (or Mukeng Zhuhai) in Anhui Province, a sea of lush, green bamboo covering about 2.3 square miles (6 sq km).

Singing Sands

While many places in China are lush and green, some…are not. About a quarter of the country is covered in deserts, including the Gobi Desert. The Gobi covers nearly 500,000 square miles (1.3 million sq km) of northern China and southern Mongolia. It's the sixth-largest desert in the world. Much of it isn't sandy. Instead, it's bare rock.

The Gobi Desert is a cold desert. There's a huge range in temperatures: from lows of about -40 degrees Fahrenheit (-40 degrees Celsius) to highs of about 113 degrees F (45 degrees C).

The Badain Jaran Desert in Alagxa has the tallest stationary sand dunes in the world. They can be more than 1,600 feet (487.7 m) tall—taller than the Empire State Building! This desert also has another unusual quality. Like a few others around the world, it has "singing sands" or "booming dunes."

They make noises, sometimes very loud noises, as if the sands are singing—or squeaking, whistling, or roaring. No one's quite sure what causes this, but it might be caused by grains of sand sliding over each other. This is just one of the weird, wonderful natural marvels of China!

The dunes of Badain Jaran Desert are quiet in the winter. In the summer, only the bigger dunes produce their unusual music.

Glossary

alkaline Containing an alkali, or matter that has a bitter taste and forms a salt when mixed with an acid.

atmospheric Relating to the atmosphere, or the mixture of gases surrounding a planet. Also, creating a certain feeling or mood.

commercialize To use something as a chance to make money.

diverse Having many different forms, types, or ideas.

ecological Having to do with ecology, or the relationship between a group of living things and their environment.

endemic Living naturally in a place.

heritage The traditions and beliefs that are a part of the history of a group or nation.

illusion Something that isn't really there or that seems different from what it is.

indigenous Having started in and coming naturally from a certain area.

kerchief A piece of cloth worn around the neck or on the head.

migration The act of an animal or people moving from one location to another.

pigment A natural coloring matter in plants and other things.

pilgrimage A journey to a holy or special place.

stalactite A pointed piece of rock that grows down from the roof of a cave.

stalagmite A pointed piece of rock that sticks up from the ground of a cave.

terrain The type of land in an area.

tributary A stream or river that flows into a larger stream, river, or lake.

UNESCO The United Nations Education, Scientific, and Cultural Organization.

For More Information

China Ministry of Culture and Tourism
6/F, B3, Ziguang Building, No 11 Huixin
Dongjie, Chaoyang District
Beijing 100029, China
(8610) 8488 3621
Website: en.chinaculture.org
Learn more about traveling to China and the country's culture at this official website.

Jiuzhai Valley (Jiuzhaigou) National Park
0837-7739753
Jiuzhai Valley Guan Li Ju,
Zhang Zha Zhen, 623402,
Aba Zhou, Sichuan, China
jiuzhaivalley@gmail.com
Website: en.jiuzhai.com/
The official website of Jiuzhaigou National Park provides lots of information, including a FAQ list, maps, photos, and tourist advice.

National Museum of China
16 E Chang'an Ave.
Dongcheng Qu, China
+86 10 6511 6400
Website: en.chnmuseum.cn
The National Museum of China is the second most-visited museum in the world. It's run by the Ministry of Culture of China and holds many artifacts related to the country and the region.

Paulson Institute
(312) 610-3710
1875 Connecticut Avenue, NW
Washington, DC 20009
Website: www.paulsoninstitute.org/conservation/national-parks/
This independent "think tank" is dedicated to fostering a China-U.S. relationship. It's working with the National Development and Reform Commission, the National Park Administration, and the Heren Foundation to create a national park system model in China.

Shilin UNESCO Global Geopark
86-871-67711439
Shilin Town, Shilin County 650000, China
Website: shilingeopark.com/public/park/zh-CHS/index.html
The official website of Shilin Geopark provides information about the area in English and Chinese.

UNESCO Headquarters
7, place de Fontenoy, 75007
Paris, France
+33 (0) 1 45 68 10 00
Website: en.unesco.org
UNESCO is the United Nations Education, Scientific, and Cultural Organization. Among other things, it maintains a list of World Heritage sites.

Zhangjiajie National Park
8C8M+4WC, Wulingyuan District
Zhangjiajie, Hunan, China
Website: zjjnfp.com
The official website for Zhangjiajie National Park features many photos and advice for visiting the park.

For Further Reading

Badger, Giles, and others. *Wild China: Natural Wonders of the World's Most Enigmatic Land.* New Haven, CT: Yale University Press, 2008.

Captivating History. *Ancient China.* Independently published: Captivating History, 2019.

Charles River Editors. *The Gobi Desert.* Charles River Press, 2018.

Chartwell Books. *World's Greatest Wonders.* New York, NY: Chartwell, 2020.

DK. *Natural Wonders of the World.* New York, NY: DK Publishing, 2017.

Editors of National Geographic. *Mount Everest.* Washington, DC: National Geographic, 2022.

Fuller, Taylor. *The Rainbow Atlas: A Guide to the World's 500 Most Colorful Places.* San Francisco, CA: Chronicle Books, 2020.

Joy, Mary Merwids. *Zhangye National Geopark China Photography.* Independently published, 2022.

Mostern, Ruth. *The Yellow River: A Natural and Unnatural History.* New Haven, CT: Yale University Press, 2021.

National Geographic Society. *National Geographic Visual Atlas of the World.* Washington, DC: National Geographic, 2017.

Sassmannshausen, Katja. *China. (Spectacular Places.)* Paris, France: Koenemann, 2020.

Bibliography

"Bird Island." *Lonely Planet.* www.lonelyplanet.com/china/qinghai-lake/attractions/bird-island/a/poi-sig/1438818/1339802

"China's Supercaves." *National Geographic.* www.nationalgeographic.com/china-caves/supercaves/

CPilgrim. "Booming Dunes of Barain Jaran Desert." *Atlas Obscura.* August 18, 2013. www.atlasobscura.com/places/booming-dunes-badain-desert

ErezSpeiser. "Tiger Leaping Gorge." *Atlas Obscura.* August 30, 2020. www.atlasobscura.com/places/tiger-leaping-gorge

EricGrundhauser. "Red Beach." *Atlas Obscura.* December 31, 2014. www.atlasobscura.com/places/red-beach

"15 Spectacular Natural Wonders of China." *Travel China Guide.* April 13, 2021. www.travelchinaguide.com/tour/natural-wonders-of-china.htm

"Forest of Ten Thousand Peaks." *Travel China Guide.* November 28, 2019. www.travelchinaguide.com/attraction/guizhou/buyi/ten-thousand-peaks-forest.htm

"Furong Cave." *Lonely Planet.* www.lonelyplanet.com/china/wulong/attractions/furong-cave/a/poi-sig/1540485/1339991

leiris. "Shilin Stone Forest." *Atlas Obscura.* March 22, 2011. www.atlasobscura.com/places/shilin-stone-forest

Jacobson, Molly McBride. "Zhangjiajie Glass Bridge." *Atlas Obscura.* September 22, 2016. www.atlasobscura.com/places/worlds-longest-glass-bridge

"Jiuzhaigou National Park." *Global Alliance of National Parks.* national-parks.org/china/jiuzhaigou

Kiprop, Victor. "The Most Extreme Points of China." *World Atlas.* May 30, 2018. www.worldatlas.com/articles/the-most-extreme-points-of-china.html

lewblank. "Avatar Hallelujah Mountain." *Atlas Obscura.* May 23, 2016. www.atlasobscura.com/places/avatar-hallelujah-mountain

"Mount Huangshan." *UNESCO World Heritage Convention.* whc.unesco.org/en/list/547/

"Mukeng Bamboo Forest." *China Discovery.* www.chinadiscovery.com/anhui/huangshan/mukeng-bamboo-forest.html

Patowary, Kaushik. "Panjin Red Beach, China." *Amusing Planet.* November 18, 2011. www.amusingplanet.com/2011/11/panjin-red-beach-china.html

Richardson, Jennifer. "20 Spectacular Nature Wonders in China That You Have to See to Believe." *Fodor's Travel.* May 1, 2019. www.fodors.com/world/asia/china/experiences/news/20-spectacular-natural-wonders-in-china-that-you-have-to-see-to-believe

Russell, Calum. "How 'Avatar' Utilizes China's Incredible Zhangjiajie National Forest Park." *Far Out Magazine.* August 15, 2022. faroutmagazine.co.uk/avatar-utilises-china-zhangjiajie-national-forest-park/

"The Sea of Bamboos: The Largest Bamboo Forest in the World." *CGTN.* January 17, 2020. news.cgtn.com/news/2020-01-17/The-Sea-of-Bamboos-The-largest-bamboo-forest-in-the-world

"Shilin UNESCO Global Geopark." *UNESCO World Heritage Convention.* en.unesco.org/global-geoparks/shilin

Song, Candice. "Zhangjiajie National Park." *China Highlights.* July 29, 2022. www.chinahighlights.com/zhangjiajie/attraction/zhangjiajie-national-forest-park.htm

"South China Karst." *UNESCO World Heritage Convention.* whc.unesco.org/en/list/1248/

"Stone Forest." *Lonely Planet.* www.lonelyplanet.com/china/yunnan/central-yunnan/attractions/stone-forest/a/poi-sig/1627667/356151

"Three Parallel Rivers of Yunnan Protected Areas." *UNESCO World Heritage* Convention. whc.unesco.org/en/list/1083/

"Top 10 Best Natural Beauty in China." *China Discovery.* www.chinadiscovery.com/articles/top-10-best-natural-beauty-in-china.html

Traverso, Vittoria. "Found: A Plant Bonanza Hidden in China's Caves." *Atlas Obscura.* February 8, 2018. www.atlasobscura.com/articles/china-caves-plants-deforestation-refuge

"Yangshuo." *Lonely Planet.* www.lonelyplanet.com/china/guangxi/yangshuo

Ye, Yvaine. "China's Spectacular Rainbow Lake Disguises Trouble Below the Surface." *New Scientist.* August 29, 2018. www.newscientist.com/article/mg23931932-400-chinas-spectacular-rainbow-lake-disguises-trouble-below-the-surface/

Index